I am Doing This for Myself

© 2020 Nimerian Fitness
All rights reserved | Contact: Nimerianfitness@gmail.com

My Starting Point

CHEST _____

WAIST _____

HIP _____

THIGH _____

CALF _____

WEIGHT _____

What made you decide to start this journey?

....

....

Rate your self-esteem and confidence today on a scale of 1 to 10

1 2 3 4 5 6 7 8 9 10

Setting Goals

Goal 1

....
....

Why do i want to achieve this goal?

....
....

Goal 2

....
....

Why do i want to achieve this goal?

....
....

Goal 3

....
....

Why do i want to achieve this goal?

....
....

WEEK Nº: ...

DAYS ON PLAN
....

Weekly Goals

☐ _____

☐ _____

☐ _____

How i'm Feeling

_____

Any Challenges This Week | Reasons To Keep Going

Weekly To-Do Checklist

☐ Weigh in ☐ Make a Menu Plan
☐ Take Measurements ☐ Try a New Recipe
☐ Take Progress Pics ☐ Have Some Me Time

> *Some people want it to happen. Some wish it would happen. Others make it happen.* – Michael Jordan

Breakfast

Lunch

Water

Dinner

Snacks

Caffeine

Steps

Activity / Exercise

Sleep

Mood

| 1 | 2 | 3 | 4 | 5 |
| 6 | 7 | 8 | 9 | 10 |

Cravings/Response

Weight

Today i'm Grateful For

How to Make Tomorrow Better

> *She was powerful not because she wasn't scared but because she went on so strongly, despite the fear.* – Atticus

Breakfast

Lunch

Water

Caffeine

Dinner

Snacks

Steps

Sleep

Activity / Exercise

Mood

| 1 | 2 | 3 | 4 | 5 |
| 6 | 7 | 8 | 9 | 10 |

Cravings/Response

Weight

Today i'm Grateful For

How to Make Tomorrow Better

> *Just keep taking chances and having fun.*
> *-Garth Brooks*

Breakfast

Lunch

Water

Dinner

Snacks

Caffeine

Steps

Activity / Exercise

Sleep

Mood

| 1 | 2 | 3 | 4 | 5 |
| 6 | 7 | 8 | 9 | 10 |

Cravings/Response

Weight

Today i'm Grateful For

How to Make Tomorrow Better

> *Fitness is like marriage. You can't cheat on it and expect it to work.*
> — Bonnie Pfiester

Breakfast

Lunch

Dinner

Snacks

Activity / Exercise

Cravings/Response

Today i'm Grateful For

How to Make Tomorrow Better

Water

Caffeine

Steps

Sleep

Mood

| 1 | 2 | 3 | 4 | 5 |
| 6 | 7 | 8 | 9 | 10 |

Weight

> It's going to be a journey. It's not a sprint to get in shape.
> – Kerri Walsh Jennings

Breakfast   Lunch

Water

Dinner   Snacks

Caffeine

Steps

Activity / Exercise

Sleep

Mood

| 1 | 2 | 3 | 4 | 5 |
| 6 | 7 | 8 | 9 | 10 |

Cravings/Response   Weight

Today i'm Grateful For  How to Make Tomorrow Better

> *When you feel like quitting, think about why you started — Anonymous.*

Breakfast

Lunch

Water

Caffeine

Dinner

Snacks

Steps

Activity / Exercise

Sleep

Mood

| 1 | 2 | 3 | 4 | 5 |
| 6 | 7 | 8 | 9 | 10 |

Cravings/Response

Weight

Today i'm Grateful For

How to Make Tomorrow Better

> *My weight does not determine my worth.*
> *— Kristin Oja*

Breakfast

Lunch

Water

Dinner

Snacks

Caffeine

Steps

Activity / Exercise

Sleep

Mood

| 1 | 2 | 3 | 4 | 5 |
| 6 | 7 | 8 | 9 | 10 |

Cravings/Response

Weight

Today i'm Grateful For

How to Make Tomorrow Better

WEEK Nº: ...

DAYS ON PLAN

....

Weekly Goals

☐ _____

☐ _____

☐ _____

How i'm Feeling

_____

_____

_____

Any Challenges This Week	Reasons To Keep Going

Weekly To-Do Checklist

☐ Weigh in   ☐ Make a Menu Plan
☐ Take Measurements   ☐ Try a New Recipe
☐ Take Progress Pics   ☐ Have Some Me Time

> I am a better person when I have less on my plate.
> – Elizabeth Gilbert

Breakfast

Lunch

Water

Dinner

Snacks

Caffeine

Steps

Activity / Exercise

Sleep

Mood

| 1 | 2 | 3 | 4 | 5 |
| 6 | 7 | 8 | 9 | 10 |

Cravings/Response

Weight

Today i'm Grateful For

How to Make Tomorrow Better

> *If you wait, all that happens is you get older.*
> — Larry McMurtry

Breakfast

Lunch

Water

Dinner

Snacks

Caffeine

Steps

Activity / Exercise

Sleep

Mood

| 1 | 2 | 3 | 4 | 5 |
| 6 | 7 | 8 | 9 | 10 |

Cravings/Response

Weight

Today i'm Grateful For

How to Make Tomorrow Better

> *You miss 100 percent of the shots you never take.*
> *— Wayne Gretzky*

Breakfast

Lunch

Water

Caffeine

Dinner

Snacks

Steps

Sleep

Activity / Exercise

Mood

| 1 | 2 | 3 | 4 | 5 |
| 6 | 7 | 8 | 9 | 10 |

Cravings/Response

Weight

Today i'm Grateful For

How to Make Tomorrow Better

> *If you don't do what's best for your body,
> you're the one who comes up on the short end.* — Julius Erving

Breakfast

Lunch

Water

Dinner

Snacks

Caffeine

Steps

Activity / Exercise

Sleep

Mood

1	2	3	4	5
6	7	8	9	10

Cravings/Response

Weight

Today i'm Grateful For

How to Make Tomorrow Better

> *If you keep good food in your fridge, you will eat good food.*
> — Errick McAdams

Breakfast

Lunch

Water

Caffeine

Dinner

Snacks

Steps

Sleep

Activity / Exercise

Mood

| 1 | 2 | 3 | 4 | 5 |
| 6 | 7 | 8 | 9 | 10 |

Cravings/Response

Weight

Today i'm Grateful For

How to Make Tomorrow Better

> *Let food be thy medicine, and medicine be thy food.*
> *— Hippocrates*

Breakfast

Lunch

Dinner

Snacks

Activity / Exercise

Cravings/Response

Water

Caffeine

Steps

Sleep

Mood

| 1 | 2 | 3 | 4 | 5 |
| 6 | 7 | 8 | 9 | 10 |

Weight

Today i'm Grateful For

How to Make Tomorrow Better

> *New meal; fresh start.*
> — Michelle Hyman

Breakfast

Lunch

Water

Dinner

Snacks

Caffeine

Steps

Activity / Exercise

Sleep

Mood

| 1 | 2 | 3 | 4 | 5 |
| 6 | 7 | 8 | 9 | 10 |

Cravings/Response

Weight

Today i'm Grateful For

How to Make Tomorrow Better

WEEK N°: ...

DAYS ON PLAN
....

Weekly Goals

- [ ]
- [ ]
- [ ]

How i'm Feeling

Any Challenges This Week | Reasons To Keep Going

Weekly To-Do Checklist

- [ ] Weigh in
- [ ] Take Measurements
- [ ] Take Progress Pics
- [ ] Make a Menu Plan
- [ ] Try a New Recipe
- [ ] Have Some Me Time

> *Never eat more than you can lift.*
> — Miss Piggy

Breakfast

Lunch

Dinner

Snacks

Activity / Exercise

Cravings/Response

Water

Caffeine

Steps

Sleep

Mood

| 1 | 2 | 3 | 4 | 5 |
| 6 | 7 | 8 | 9 | 10 |

Weight

Today i'm Grateful For

How to Make Tomorrow Better

> *Food can be both enjoyable and nourishing.*
> *— Alyssa Ardolino*

Breakfast

Lunch

Dinner

Snacks

Activity / Exercise

Cravings/Response

Water

Caffeine

Steps

Sleep

Mood

1	2	3	4	5
6	7	8	9	10

Weight

Today i'm Grateful For

How to Make Tomorrow Better

> *If I don't eat junk, I don't gain weight.*
> *– Paula Christensen*

Breakfast

Lunch

Dinner

Snacks

Activity / Exercise

Cravings/Response

Water

Caffeine

Steps

Sleep

Mood

| 1 | 2 | 3 | 4 | 5 |
| 6 | 7 | 8 | 9 | 10 |

Weight

Today i'm Grateful For

How to Make Tomorrow Better

> *The only way to lose weight is to check it in as airline baggage.*
> — Peggy Ryan

Breakfast

Lunch

Dinner

Snacks

Activity / Exercise

Cravings/Response

Water

Caffeine

Steps

Sleep

Mood

| 1 | 2 | 3 | 4 | 5 |
| 6 | 7 | 8 | 9 | 10 |

Weight

Today i'm Grateful For

How to Make Tomorrow Better

"It would be far easier to lose weight permanently if replacement parts weren't so handy in the refrigerator." – Hugh Allen

Breakfast

Lunch

Dinner

Snacks

Activity / Exercise

Cravings/Response

Water

Caffeine

Steps

Sleep

Mood

| 1 | 2 | 3 | 4 | 5 |
| 6 | 7 | 8 | 9 | 10 |

Weight

Today i'm Grateful For

How to Make Tomorrow Better

> A diet is when you watch what you eat and wish you could eat what you watch. – Hermione Gingold

Breakfast

Lunch

Dinner

Snacks

Activity / Exercise

Cravings/Response

Today i'm Grateful For

How to Make Tomorrow Better

Water

Caffeine

Steps

Sleep

Mood

| 1 | 2 | 3 | 4 | 5 |
| 6 | 7 | 8 | 9 | 10 |

Weight

> Keep an open mind and a closed refrigerator.
> – Anonymous

Breakfast

Lunch

Water

Dinner

Snacks

Caffeine

Steps

Activity / Exercise

Sleep

Mood

| 1 | 2 | 3 | 4 | 5 |
| 6 | 7 | 8 | 9 | 10 |

Cravings/Response

Weight

Today i'm Grateful For

How to Make Tomorrow Better

WEEK N°: ...

DAYS ON PLAN
....

Weekly Goals

- [ ]
- [ ]
- [ ]

How i'm Feeling

Any Challenges This Week

Reasons To Keep Going

Weekly To-Do Checklist

- [ ] Weigh in
- [ ] Take Measurements
- [ ] Take Progress Pics
- [ ] Make a Menu Plan
- [ ] Try a New Recipe
- [ ] Have Some Me Time

> I choose self-care.
> — Alyssa Ardolino

Breakfast

Lunch

Water

Dinner

Snacks

Caffeine

Steps

Activity / Exercise

Sleep

Mood

| 1 | 2 | 3 | 4 | 5 |
| 6 | 7 | 8 | 9 | 10 |

Cravings/Response

Weight

Today i'm Grateful For

How to Make Tomorrow Better

> *My favorite exercise is a cross between a lunge and a crunch.*
> *I call it lunch.* — Anonymous

Breakfast

Lunch

Dinner

Snacks

Activity / Exercise

Cravings/Response

Water

Caffeine

Steps

Sleep

Mood

| 1 | 2 | 3 | 4 | 5 |
| 6 | 7 | 8 | 9 | 10 |

Weight

Today i'm Grateful For

How to Make Tomorrow Better

> Today I bought a cupcake without the sprinkles. Diets are hard.
> — Author Unknown

Breakfast

Lunch

Water

Caffeine

Dinner

Snacks

Steps

Sleep

Activity / Exercise

Mood

| 1 | 2 | 3 | 4 | 5 |
| 6 | 7 | 8 | 9 | 10 |

Cravings/Response

Weight

Today i'm Grateful For

How to Make Tomorrow Better

> *Only I can change my life. No one can do it for me.*
> *— Anonymous*

Breakfast

Lunch

Dinner

Snacks

Activity / Exercise

Cravings/Response

Water

Caffeine

Steps

Sleep

Mood

| 1 | 2 | 3 | 4 | 5 |
| 6 | 7 | 8 | 9 | 10 |

Weight

Today i'm Grateful For

How to Make Tomorrow Better

> "Weight loss doesn't begin in the gym with a dumbbell; it starts in your head with a decision." – Toni Sorenson

Breakfast

Lunch

Water

Dinner

Snacks

Caffeine

Steps

Activity / Exercise

Sleep

Mood

| 1 | 2 | 3 | 4 | 5 |
| 6 | 7 | 8 | 9 | 10 |

Cravings/Response

Weight

Today i'm Grateful For

How to Make Tomorrow Better

> *Just believe in yourself. Even if you don't, pretend that you do, and at some point, you will.* — Venus Williams

Breakfast

Lunch

Dinner

Snacks

Activity / Exercise

Cravings/Response

Water

Caffeine

Steps

Sleep

Mood

| 1 | 2 | 3 | 4 | 5 |
| 6 | 7 | 8 | 9 | 10 |

Weight

Today i'm Grateful For

How to Make Tomorrow Better

> I always believed if you take care of your body it will take care of you.
> – Ted Lindsay

Breakfast

Lunch

Water

Dinner

Snacks

Caffeine

Steps

Activity / Exercise

Sleep

Mood

| 1 | 2 | 3 | 4 | 5 |
| 6 | 7 | 8 | 9 | 10 |

Cravings/Response

Weight

Today i'm Grateful For

How to Make Tomorrow Better

WEEK N°: ...

DAYS ON PLAN

....

Weekly Goals

- [ ]
- [ ]
- [ ]

How i'm Feeling

Any Challenges This Week | Reasons To Keep Going

Weekly To-Do Checklist

- [ ] Weigh in
- [ ] Take Measurements
- [ ] Take Progress Pics
- [ ] Make a Menu Plan
- [ ] Try a New Recipe
- [ ] Have Some Me Time

> *Unless you puke, faint, or die, keep going!*
> *— Jillian Michaels*

Breakfast

Lunch

Dinner

Snacks

Activity / Exercise

Cravings/Response

Water

Caffeine

Steps

Sleep

Mood

1	2	3	4	5
6	7	8	9	10

Weight

Today i'm Grateful For

How to Make Tomorrow Better

> *Triumph by putting a little soul into it!*
> — Nancy Mure

Breakfast

Lunch

Water

Dinner

Snacks

Caffeine

Steps

Activity / Exercise

Sleep

Mood

| 1 | 2 | 3 | 4 | 5 |
| 6 | 7 | 8 | 9 | 10 |

Cravings/Response

Weight

Today i'm Grateful For

How to Make Tomorrow Better

> *Success is the sum of small efforts — repeated day-in and day-out.*
> *– Robert Collier*

Breakfast

Lunch

Water

Dinner

Snacks

Caffeine

Steps

Activity / Exercise

Sleep

Mood

| 1 | 2 | 3 | 4 | 5 |
| 6 | 7 | 8 | 9 | 10 |

Cravings/Response

Weight

Today i'm Grateful For

How to Make Tomorrow Better

> It is better to take small steps in the right direction than to make a great leap forward only to stumble backward.

Breakfast

Lunch

Water

Dinner

Snacks

Caffeine

Steps

Activity / Exercise

Sleep

Mood

| 1 | 2 | 3 | 4 | 5 |
| 6 | 7 | 8 | 9 | 10 |

Cravings/Response

Weight

Today i'm Grateful For

How to Make Tomorrow Better

> *The mind is everything. What you think you become.*
> *— Buddha*

Breakfast

Lunch

Dinner

Snacks

Activity / Exercise

Cravings/Response

Water

Caffeine

Steps

Sleep

Mood

| 1 | 2 | 3 | 4 | 5 |
| 6 | 7 | 8 | 9 | 10 |

Weight

Today i'm Grateful For

How to Make Tomorrow Better

> *To give anything less than your best is to sacrifice the gift.*
> *– Steve Prefontaine*

Breakfast

Lunch

Dinner

Snacks

Activity / Exercise

Cravings/Response

Water

Caffeine

Steps

Sleep

Mood

| 1 | 2 | 3 | 4 | 5 |
| 6 | 7 | 8 | 9 | 10 |

Weight

Today i'm Grateful For

How to Make Tomorrow Better

> *Looking after my health today gives me a better hope for tomorrow.*
> *— Anne Wilson Schaef*

Breakfast

Lunch

Water

Dinner

Snacks

Caffeine

Steps

Activity / Exercise

Sleep

Mood

| 1 | 2 | 3 | 4 | 5 |
| 6 | 7 | 8 | 9 | 10 |

Cravings/Response

Weight

Today i'm Grateful For

How to Make Tomorrow Better

WEEK N°: ...

DAYS ON PLAN

....

Weekly Goals

- [ ] _____
- [ ] _____
- [ ] _____

How i'm Feeling

_____

Any Challenges This Week	Reasons To Keep Going

Weekly To-Do Checklist

- [ ] Weigh in
- [ ] Take Measurements
- [ ] Take Progress Pics
- [ ] Make a Menu Plan
- [ ] Try a New Recipe
- [ ] Have Some Me Time

> *The scale is merely a measure of my relationship with gravity.*
> — Lauren Harris-Pincus

Breakfast

Lunch

Water

Dinner

Snacks

Caffeine

Steps

Activity / Exercise

Sleep

Mood

| 1 | 2 | 3 | 4 | 5 |
| 6 | 7 | 8 | 9 | 10 |

Cravings/Response

Weight

Today i'm Grateful For

How to Make Tomorrow Better

> *Eliminate the mindset of can't — because you can do anything.*
> *— Toni Horton*

Breakfast

Lunch

Water

Dinner

Snacks

Caffeine

Steps

Activity / Exercise

Sleep

Mood

| 1 | 2 | 3 | 4 | 5 |
| 6 | 7 | 8 | 9 | 10 |

Cravings/Response

Weight

Today i'm Grateful For

How to Make Tomorrow Better

> *Exercise should be regarded as a tribute to the heart.*
> *— Gene Tunney*

Breakfast

Lunch

Water

Dinner

Snacks

Caffeine

Steps

Activity / Exercise

Sleep

Mood

| 1 | 2 | 3 | 4 | 5 |
| 6 | 7 | 8 | 9 | 10 |

Cravings/Response

Weight

Today i'm Grateful For

How to Make Tomorrow Better

> *Wisdom is doing now what you are going to be happy with later on.*
> *— Joyce Meyer*

Breakfast

Lunch

Dinner

Snacks

Activity / Exercise

Cravings/Response

Water

Caffeine

Steps

Sleep

Mood

1	2	3	4	5
6	7	8	9	10

Weight

Today i'm Grateful For

How to Make Tomorrow Better

> *Decide. Commit. Succeed.*
> *— Justin Seedman*

Breakfast

Lunch

Water

Caffeine

Dinner

Snacks

Steps

Activity / Exercise

Sleep

Mood

| 1 | 2 | 3 | 4 | 5 |
| 6 | 7 | 8 | 9 | 10 |

Cravings/Response

Weight

Today i'm Grateful For

How to Make Tomorrow Better

> "Don't work out because you hate your body, work out because you love it."
> — Anonymous

Breakfast

Lunch

Water

Dinner

Snacks

Caffeine

Steps

Activity / Exercise

Sleep

Mood

| 1 | 2 | 3 | 4 | 5 |
| 6 | 7 | 8 | 9 | 10 |

Cravings/Response

Weight

Today i'm Grateful For

How to Make Tomorrow Better

> *Strength does not come from what you can do. It comes from overcoming the things you once thought you couldn't.* –Nikki Rogers

Breakfast

Lunch

Water

Dinner

Snacks

Caffeine

Steps

Activity / Exercise

Sleep

Mood

| 1 | 2 | 3 | 4 | 5 |
| 6 | 7 | 8 | 9 | 10 |

Cravings/Response

Weight

Today i'm Grateful For

How to Make Tomorrow Better

WEEK N°: ...

DAYS ON PLAN

....

Weekly Goals

☐ _____

☐ _____

☐ _____

How i'm Feeling

_____
_____
_____
_____

Any Challenges This Week	Reasons To Keep Going

Weekly To-Do Checklist

☐ Weigh in   ☐ Make a Menu Plan

☐ Take Measurements   ☐ Try a New Recipe

☐ Take Progress Pics ☐ Have Some Me Time

> *Eliminate the mindset of can't — because you can do anything.*
> *— Tony Horton*

Breakfast

Lunch

Water

Dinner

Snacks

Caffeine

Steps

Activity / Exercise

Sleep

Mood

| 1 | 2 | 3 | 4 | 5 |
| 6 | 7 | 8 | 9 | 10 |

Cravings/Response

Weight

Today i'm Grateful For

How to Make Tomorrow Better

> *Make time for it. Just get it done. Nobody ever got strong or got in shape by thinking about it. They did it.* — Jim Wendler

Breakfast

Lunch

Dinner

Snacks

Activity / Exercise

Cravings/Response

Water

Caffeine

Steps

Sleep

Mood

| 1 | 2 | 3 | 4 | 5 |
| 6 | 7 | 8 | 9 | 10 |

Weight

Today i'm Grateful For

How to Make Tomorrow Better

> *The groundwork of all happiness is health.*
> *— Leigh Hunt*

Breakfast

Lunch

Dinner

Snacks

Activity / Exercise

Cravings/Response

Water

Caffeine

Steps

Sleep

Mood

| 1 | 2 | 3 | 4 | 5 |
| 6 | 7 | 8 | 9 | 10 |

Weight

Today i'm Grateful For

How to Make Tomorrow Better

> *It has to be hard so you'll never ever forget.*
> *— Bob Harper*

Breakfast

Lunch

Water

Dinner

Snacks

Caffeine

Steps

Activity / Exercise

Sleep

Mood

| 1 | 2 | 3 | 4 | 5 |
| 6 | 7 | 8 | 9 | 10 |

Cravings/Response

Weight

Today i'm Grateful For

How to Make Tomorrow Better

> *If you have discipline, drive, and determination... nothing is impossible.*
> — Dana Linn Bailey

Breakfast   Lunch

Water

Dinner   Snacks

Caffeine

Steps

Activity / Exercise

Sleep

Mood

| 1 | 2 | 3 | 4 | 5 |
| 6 | 7 | 8 | 9 | 10 |

Cravings/Response

Weight

Today i'm Grateful For   How to Make Tomorrow Better

> If you have discipline, drive, and determination ...
> nothing is impossible.— Dana Linn Bailey

Breakfast

Lunch

Dinner

Snacks

Water

Caffeine

Steps

Activity / Exercise

Sleep

Mood

| 1 | 2 | 3 | 4 | 5 |
| 6 | 7 | 8 | 9 | 10 |

Cravings/Response

Weight

Today i'm Grateful For

How to Make Tomorrow Better

> *Weight loss doesn't begin in the gym with a dumb bell; it starts in your head with a decision.* — Toni Sorenson

Breakfast

Lunch

Water

Caffeine

Dinner

Snacks

Steps

Activity / Exercise

Sleep

Mood

| 1 | 2 | 3 | 4 | 5 |
| 6 | 7 | 8 | 9 | 10 |

Cravings/Response

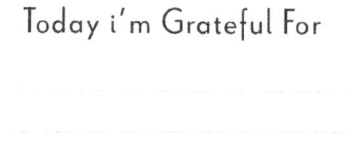

Weight

Today i'm Grateful For

How to Make Tomorrow Better

WEEK N°: ...

DAYS ON PLAN

....

Weekly Goals

- [ ]
- [ ]
- [ ]

How i'm Feeling

Any Challenges This Week

Reasons To Keep Going

Weekly To-Do Checklist

- [ ] Weigh in
- [ ] Take Measurements
- [ ] Take Progress Pics
- [ ] Make a Menu Plan
- [ ] Try a New Recipe
- [ ] Have Some Me Time

> *You didn't gain all your weight in one day; you won't lose it in one day. Be patient with yourself.* — Jenna Wolfe

Breakfast

Lunch

Water

Dinner

Snacks

Caffeine

Steps

Activity / Exercise

Sleep

Mood

| 1 | 2 | 3 | 4 | 5 |
| 6 | 7 | 8 | 9 | 10 |

Cravings/Response

Weight

Today i'm Grateful For

How to Make Tomorrow Better

> *Make time for it. Just get it done. Nobody ever got strong or got in shape by thinking about it. They did it.* — Jim Wendler

Breakfast

Lunch

Dinner

Snacks

Activity / Exercise

Cravings/Response

Water

Caffeine

Steps

Sleep

Mood

| 1 | 2 | 3 | 4 | 5 |
| 6 | 7 | 8 | 9 | 10 |

Weight

Today i'm Grateful For

How to Make Tomorrow Better

> *Most people give up right before the big break comes, don't let that person be you.* – Michael Boyle

Breakfast

Lunch

Water

Dinner

Snacks

Caffeine

Steps

Activity / Exercise

Sleep

Mood

| 1 | 2 | 3 | 4 | 5 |
| 6 | 7 | 8 | 9 | 10 |

Cravings/Response

Weight

Today i'm Grateful For

How to Make Tomorrow Better

> *Just believe in yourself. Even if you don't, pretend that you do and, at some point, you will.* — Venus Williams

Breakfast

Lunch

Water

Dinner

Snacks

Caffeine

Steps

Activity / Exercise

Sleep

Mood

| 1 | 2 | 3 | 4 | 5 |
| 6 | 7 | 8 | 9 | 10 |

Cravings/Response

Weight

Today i'm Grateful For

How to Make Tomorrow Better

> *If it doesn't challenge you, it doesn't change you.*
> — Jenna Wolfe

Breakfast

Lunch

Dinner

Snacks

Activity / Exercise

Cravings/Response

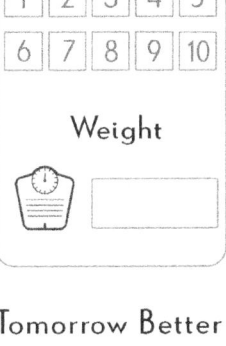

Water

Caffeine

Steps

Sleep

Mood

1	2	3	4	5
6	7	8	9	10

Weight

Today i'm Grateful For

How to Make Tomorrow Better

> *Nobody is perfect, so get over the fear of being or doing everything perfectly. Besides, perfect is boring.* — Jillian Michaels

Breakfast

Lunch

Dinner

Snacks

Activity / Exercise

Cravings/Response

Water

Caffeine

Steps

Sleep

Mood

1 2 3 4 5
6 7 8 9 10

Weight

Today i'm Grateful For

How to Make Tomorrow Better

> *Exercise should be regarded as a tribute to the heart.*
> *— Gene Tunney*

Breakfast

Lunch

Water

Dinner

Snacks

Caffeine

Steps

Activity / Exercise

Sleep

Mood

| 1 | 2 | 3 | 4 | 5 |
| 6 | 7 | 8 | 9 | 10 |

Cravings/Response

Weight

Today i'm Grateful For

How to Make Tomorrow Better

WEEK N°: ...

DAYS ON PLAN

....

Weekly Goals

- [ ]
- [ ]
- [ ]

How i'm Feeling

Any Challenges This Week | Reasons To Keep Going

Weekly To-Do Checklist

- [ ] Weigh in
- [ ] Take Measurements
- [ ] Take Progress Pics
- [ ] Make a Menu Plan
- [ ] Try a New Recipe
- [ ] Have Some Me Time

> *To improve is to change; to be perfect is to change often.*
> *— Winston Churchill*

Breakfast

Lunch

Water

Dinner

Snacks

Caffeine

Steps

Activity / Exercise

Sleep

Mood

| 1 | 2 | 3 | 4 | 5 |
| 6 | 7 | 8 | 9 | 10 |

Cravings/Response

Weight

Today i'm Grateful For

How to Make Tomorrow Better

> *I always believed if you take care of your body it will take care of you.*
> *— Ted Lindsay*

Breakfast

Lunch

Dinner

Snacks

Activity / Exercise

Cravings/Response

Water

Caffeine

Steps

Sleep

Mood

1	2	3	4	5
6	7	8	9	10

Weight

Today i'm Grateful For

How to Make Tomorrow Better

> *Ability is what you're capable of doing. Motivation determines what you do. Attitude determines how well you do it.* – Lou Holtz

Breakfast

Lunch

Water

Dinner

Snacks

Caffeine

Steps

Activity / Exercise

Sleep

Mood

| 1 | 2 | 3 | 4 | 5 |
| 6 | 7 | 8 | 9 | 10 |

Cravings/Response

Weight

Today i'm Grateful For

How to Make Tomorrow Better

> "You may be disappointed if you fail, but you are doomed if you don't try."
> — Beverly Sills

Breakfast

Lunch

Dinner

Snacks

Activity / Exercise

Cravings/Response

Water

Caffeine

Steps

Sleep

Mood

| 1 | 2 | 3 | 4 | 5 |
| 6 | 7 | 8 | 9 | 10 |

Weight

Today i'm Grateful For

How to Make Tomorrow Better

> *Looking after my health today gives me a better hope for tomorrow*
> *— Anne Wilson Schaef*

Breakfast

Lunch

Dinner

Snacks

Activity / Exercise

Cravings/Response

Water

Caffeine

Steps

Sleep

Mood

| 1 | 2 | 3 | 4 | 5 |
| 6 | 7 | 8 | 9 | 10 |

Weight

Today i'm Grateful For

How to Make Tomorrow Better

> If you don't do what's best for your body, you're the one who comes up on the short end. – Julius Erving

Breakfast

Lunch

Dinner

Snacks

Activity / Exercise

Cravings/Response

Water

Caffeine

Steps

Sleep

Mood

| 1 | 2 | 3 | 4 | 5 |
| 6 | 7 | 8 | 9 | 10 |

Weight

Today i'm Grateful For

How to Make Tomorrow Better

> Lose an hour in the morning, and you will spend all day looking for it.
> – Richard Whately

Breakfast

Lunch

Water

Dinner

Snacks

Caffeine

Steps

Activity / Exercise

Sleep

Mood

| 1 | 2 | 3 | 4 | 5 |
| 6 | 7 | 8 | 9 | 10 |

Cravings/Response

Weight

Today i'm Grateful For

How to Make Tomorrow Better

WEEK N°: ...

DAYS ON PLAN

....

Weekly Goals

☐ _____

☐ _____

☐ _____

How i'm Feeling

_____

_____

_____

Any Challenges This Week	Reasons To Keep Going

Weekly To-Do Checklist

☐ Weigh in   ☐ Make a Menu Plan
☐ Take Measurements ☐ Try a New Recipe
☐ Take Progress Pics ☐ Have Some Me Time

> *I don't stop when I'm tired, I stop when I'm DONE!*

Breakfast

Lunch

Water

Caffeine

Dinner

Snacks

Steps

Activity / Exercise

Sleep

Mood

| 1 | 2 | 3 | 4 | 5 |
| 6 | 7 | 8 | 9 | 10 |

Cravings/Response

Weight

Today i'm Grateful For

How to Make Tomorrow Better

> If it was about knowledge, we would all be skinny and rich.
> It's not about what you know but what you do!

Breakfast

Lunch

Water

Dinner

Snacks

Caffeine

Steps

Activity / Exercise

Sleep

Mood

| 1 | 2 | 3 | 4 | 5 |
| 6 | 7 | 8 | 9 | 10 |

Cravings/Response

Weight

Today i'm Grateful For

How to Make Tomorrow Better

> *The distance between who am I am and who I want to be is only separated by what I do.*

Breakfast

Lunch

Dinner

Snacks

Activity / Exercise

Cravings/Response

Water

Caffeine

Steps

Sleep

Mood

| 1 | 2 | 3 | 4 | 5 |
| 6 | 7 | 8 | 9 | 10 |

Weight

Today i'm Grateful For

How to Make Tomorrow Better

> *The only bad workout is the one that didn't happen.*

Breakfast

Lunch

Water

Dinner

Snacks

Caffeine

Steps

Activity / Exercise

Sleep

Mood

| 1 | 2 | 3 | 4 | 5 |
| 6 | 7 | 8 | 9 | 10 |

Cravings/Response

Weight

Today i'm Grateful For

How to Make Tomorrow Better

> To change your body you must first change your mind.

Breakfast

Lunch

Dinner

Snacks

Activity / Exercise

Cravings/Response

Water

Caffeine

Steps

Sleep

Mood

| 1 | 2 | 3 | 4 | 5 |
| 6 | 7 | 8 | 9 | 10 |

Weight

Today i'm Grateful For

How to Make Tomorrow Better

> *Someone busier than you is running right now.*

Breakfast

Lunch

Dinner

Snacks

Water

Caffeine

Steps

Sleep

Mood

| 1 | 2 | 3 | 4 | 5 |
| 6 | 7 | 8 | 9 | 10 |

Weight

Activity / Exercise

Cravings/Response

Today i'm Grateful For

How to Make Tomorrow Better

> *Working out is never convenient. But neither is illness, diabetes and obesity!*

Breakfast

Lunch

Dinner

Snacks

Activity / Exercise

Cravings/Response

Water

Caffeine

Steps

Sleep

Mood

| 1 | 2 | 3 | 4 | 5 |
| 6 | 7 | 8 | 9 | 10 |

Weight

Today i'm Grateful For

How to Make Tomorrow Better

WEEK N°: ....

DAYS ON PLAN
....

Weekly Goals

☐ _____
_____

☐ _____
_____

☐ _____
_____

How i'm Feeling

_____
_____
_____
_____

Any Challenges This Week	Reasons To Keep Going

Weekly To-Do Checklist

☐ Weigh in   ☐ Make a Menu Plan
☐ Take Measurements   ☐ Try a New Recipe
☐ Take Progress Pics   ☐ Have Some Me Time

> *You can't run from all your problems, but it will help you lose weight.*

Breakfast

Lunch

Water

Caffeine

Dinner

Snacks

Steps

Sleep

Activity / Exercise

Mood

| 1 | 2 | 3 | 4 | 5 |
| 6 | 7 | 8 | 9 | 10 |

Cravings/Response

Weight

Today i'm Grateful For

How to Make Tomorrow Better

Get comfortable with being uncomfortable!

Breakfast

Lunch

Dinner

Snacks

Activity / Exercise

Cravings/Response

Water

Caffeine

Steps

Sleep

Mood

| 1 | 2 | 3 | 4 | 5 |
| 6 | 7 | 8 | 9 | 10 |

Weight

Today i'm Grateful For

How to Make Tomorrow Better

> *When it burns, is when you're just getting started.*
> *That's when you get stronger!*

Breakfast

Lunch

Dinner

Snacks

Activity / Exercise

Cravings/Response

Water

Caffeine

Steps

Sleep

Mood

| 1 | 2 | 3 | 4 | 5 |
| 6 | 7 | 8 | 9 | 10 |

Weight

Today i'm Grateful For

How to Make Tomorrow Better

> *The only way to lose weight is to check it in as airline baggage.*
> — Peggy Ryan

Breakfast

Lunch

Dinner

Snacks

Activity / Exercise

Cravings/Response

Today i'm Grateful For

How to Make Tomorrow Better

Water

Caffeine

Steps

Sleep

Mood

| 1 | 2 | 3 | 4 | 5 |
| 6 | 7 | 8 | 9 | 10 |

Weight

> *It would be far easier to lose weight permanently if replacement parts weren't so handy in the refrigerator."* – Hugh Allen

Breakfast

Lunch

Water

Dinner

Snacks

Caffeine

Steps

Activity / Exercise

Sleep

Mood

| 1 | 2 | 3 | 4 | 5 |
| 6 | 7 | 8 | 9 | 10 |

Cravings/Response

Weight

Today i'm Grateful For

How to Make Tomorrow Better

> *If you have 30 minutes for Facebook, you have 1 hour for the gym!*

Breakfast

Lunch

Dinner

Snacks

Activity / Exercise

Cravings/Response

Today i'm Grateful For

How to Make Tomorrow Better

Water

Caffeine

Steps

Sleep

Mood

| 1 | 2 | 3 | 4 | 5 |
| 6 | 7 | 8 | 9 | 10 |

Weight

> *The best way to predict your health is to create it.*

Breakfast

Lunch

Water

Dinner

Snacks

Caffeine

Steps

Activity / Exercise

Sleep

Mood

| 1 | 2 | 3 | 4 | 5 |
| 6 | 7 | 8 | 9 | 10 |

Cravings/Response

Weight

Today i'm Grateful For

How to Make Tomorrow Better

WEEK N°: ...

DAYS ON PLAN
....

Weekly Goals

☐ ....

☐ ....

☐ ....

How i'm Feeling

Any Challenges This Week | Reasons To Keep Going

Weekly To-Do Checklist

☐ Weigh in					☐ Make a Menu Plan
☐ Take Measurements		☐ Try a New Recipe
☐ Take Progress Pics		☐ Have Some Me Time

> *On the other side of your workout is the body and health you want!*

Breakfast

Lunch

Water

Dinner

Snacks

Caffeine

Steps

Activity / Exercise

Sleep

Mood

| 1 | 2 | 3 | 4 | 5 |
| 6 | 7 | 8 | 9 | 10 |

Cravings/Response

Weight

Today i'm Grateful For

How to Make Tomorrow Better

> *Get started as if you are motivated.*
> *Pretend. And the motivation will come!*

Breakfast

Lunch

Water

Dinner

Snacks

Caffeine

Steps

Activity / Exercise

Sleep

Mood

| 1 | 2 | 3 | 4 | 5 |
| 6 | 7 | 8 | 9 | 10 |

Cravings/Response

Weight

Today i'm Grateful For

How to Make Tomorrow Better

> *Excuses don't burn calories.*

Breakfast

Lunch

Water

Dinner

Snacks

Caffeine

Steps

Activity / Exercise

Sleep

Mood

| 1 | 2 | 3 | 4 | 5 |
| 6 | 7 | 8 | 9 | 10 |

Cravings/Response

Weight

Today i'm Grateful For

How to Make Tomorrow Better

> *Your body hears everything your mind says.*
> *Keep going. You can!*

Breakfast

Lunch

Water

Dinner

Snacks

Caffeine

Steps

Activity / Exercise

Sleep

Mood

| 1 | 2 | 3 | 4 | 5 |
| 6 | 7 | 8 | 9 | 10 |

Cravings/Response

Weight

Today i'm Grateful For

How to Make Tomorrow Better

> *Don't stop until you're proud.*

Breakfast

Lunch

Water

Dinner

Snacks

Caffeine

Steps

Activity / Exercise

Sleep

Mood

1	2	3	4	5
6	7	8	9	10

Cravings/Response

Weight

Today i'm Grateful For

How to Make Tomorrow Better

> *You don't have to go fast, you just have to go.*

Breakfast

Lunch

Water

Dinner

Snacks

Caffeine

Steps

Activity / Exercise

Sleep

Mood

1	2	3	4	5
6	7	8	9	10

Cravings/Response

Weight

Today i'm Grateful For

How to Make Tomorrow Better

> *If you're tired of starting over; stop giving up!*

Breakfast

Lunch

Dinner

Snacks

Activity / Exercise

Cravings/Response

Water

Caffeine

Steps

Sleep

Mood

| 1 | 2 | 3 | 4 | 5 |
| 6 | 7 | 8 | 9 | 10 |

Weight

Today i'm Grateful For

How to Make Tomorrow Better

WEEK N°: ...

DAYS ON PLAN
....

Weekly Goals

- [ ]
- [ ]
- [ ]

How i'm Feeling

Any Challenges This Week | Reasons To Keep Going

Weekly To-Do Checklist

- [ ] Weigh in
- [ ] Take Measurements
- [ ] Take Progress Pics
- [ ] Make a Menu Plan
- [ ] Try a New Recipe
- [ ] Have Some Me Time

> Weight loss is not impossible.
> Weight loss is hard, but hard is not the same as impossible.

Breakfast

Lunch

Water

Dinner

Snacks

Caffeine

Steps

Activity / Exercise

Sleep

Mood

| 1 | 2 | 3 | 4 | 5 |
| 6 | 7 | 8 | 9 | 10 |

Cravings/Response

Weight

Today i'm Grateful For

How to Make Tomorrow Better

> *The question isn't can you, it's will you!*

Breakfast

Lunch

Dinner

Snacks

Activity / Exercise

Cravings/Response

Water

Caffeine

Steps

Sleep

Mood

| 1 | 2 | 3 | 4 | 5 |
| 6 | 7 | 8 | 9 | 10 |

Weight

Today i'm Grateful For

How to Make Tomorrow Better

> *Workouts are like life. The harder it is,
> the STRONGER YOU BECOME!*

Breakfast

Lunch

Dinner

Snacks

Activity / Exercise

Cravings/Response

Water

Caffeine

Steps

Sleep

Mood

| 1 | 2 | 3 | 4 | 5 |
| 6 | 7 | 8 | 9 | 10 |

Weight

Today i'm Grateful For

How to Make Tomorrow Better

> *If no one thinks you can, then you have to!*

Breakfast

Lunch

Water

Dinner

Snacks

Caffeine

Steps

Activity / Exercise

Sleep

Mood

| 1 | 2 | 3 | 4 | 5 |
| 6 | 7 | 8 | 9 | 10 |

Cravings/Response

Weight

Today i'm Grateful For

How to Make Tomorrow Better

> If you still look good at the end of your work out...
> you didn't work hard enough!

Breakfast

Lunch

Dinner

Snacks

Activity / Exercise

Cravings/Response

Water

Caffeine

Steps

Sleep

Mood

| 1 | 2 | 3 | 4 | 5 |
| 6 | 7 | 8 | 9 | 10 |

Weight

Today i'm Grateful For

How to Make Tomorrow Better

> *If you still look good at the end of your work out...*
> *you didn't work hard enough!*

Breakfast

Lunch

Dinner

Snacks

Activity / Exercise

Cravings/Response

Water

Caffeine

Steps

Sleep

Mood

| 1 | 2 | 3 | 4 | 5 |
| 6 | 7 | 8 | 9 | 10 |

Weight

Today i'm Grateful For

How to Make Tomorrow Better

> To enjoy the glow of good health, you must exercise.

Breakfast

Lunch

Water

Dinner

Snacks

Caffeine

Steps

Activity / Exercise

Sleep

Mood

| 1 | 2 | 3 | 4 | 5 |
| 6 | 7 | 8 | 9 | 10 |

Cravings/Response

Weight

Today i'm Grateful For

How to Make Tomorrow Better

NOTES

NOTES

Made in the USA
Coppell, TX
10 December 2021